A Cookie to Go

DJ Kiggins

PAGE PUBLISHING, INC.
New York, NY

First originally published by Page Publishing 2013

ISBN 978-1-62838-026-2 (pbk)
ISBN 978-1-62838-027-9 (digital)

Printed in the United States of America

Dedication

Okay, kids. You were right: my first book and I dedicate it to our dog. How could it be any other way, dear hearts?

This is for you, Norman. I truly hope there are many, delicious cookies in Heaven. You made the last nine years of my life impossibly full and filled with fun and laughter. You added so much love to our family and your very presence increased the dimension of all of our shared experiences. I miss you so very much.

This book is also for you, dear reader:

For those who have a beloved canine pet, for those who have loved a dog more than they ever believed possible, and for those who have had to make that final and horrifying decision to release their most beloved dog back into the capable arms of whomever they believe is their God. These are simply some stories to heal your hearts and make you laugh!

Thanks to my family, Larry, Christopher, and Kerry Lynn. Christy, without you, I never would have put pen to paper to begin this book. Also, thank you to my dearest Connie, who named this book, and put up with puppy Norman. Thanks to both of my sisters: Marilyn for occasionally babysitting a very pesky puppy, Phoebe, and Terrie, who stars with her dog, Macy, in one of these hilarious stories. What can I say about Lorrie, except thanks for your friendship and the great stories you have provided interacting with your dog–yes your dog–Andy. All other generous contributions were made by close family and friends and are sincerely appreciated: Mary, Patty, Marcia and Dennis, and of course my dear Peggy. All last names have been removed to protect the guilty (that's for you Mary Margaret)! Thanks also to my patient family and friends, who simply put up with my past pets; Colleen and Rick, Judy and John, and Maggie, who always looked after all of us. Last, but never least thank you to my dearest Norman.

Introduction

This book is a compilation of stories about my dogs and the dogs I have known. These stories have been a great comfort to others who have recently lost a beloved pet. It feels good to remember and laugh! What makes these stories special is they are one hundred percent, hand-over-heart true. Every little detail actually happened. It's ironic that Norman, the reason I wrote these stories, was such a great dog he doesn't really star in many of them. He never created enough havoc to cause disarray like some of my other pets. After Norman's death a few weeks ago, I realized I needed to try and remember all the great things about his life instead of reflecting upon his last and very sad days. What came to mind was all the laughter he gave to our family.

My children loved to regale our friends with disastrous stories all filled with calamities where I would need to choose either saving them or our dog, Norman. My daughter, Kerry Lynn, was absolutely convinced that had we found ourselves in a sinking boat I would easily throw both her and her brother, Christopher, quickly overboard, in order to save him. They truly believed this and somewhere buried secretly in my heart I knew why I had spent so much money on swimming lessons for them. I was confident both of our children could swim and survive–not so, Norman. He was the only Golden Retriever I had ever met who was totally terrified of water in any form; still, moving, crashing, or wet. He would have drowned in my daughter's scenario, and I could never have lived with this.

From day one, wasn't the most wonderful aspect of your dog how he or she made you laugh? I remember the really simple examples of this as I look back on Norman's life filled with everyday antics. It was never the remarkable, but the simple actions that, remembered, truly brought me joy.

I want to thank my husband of 30 years, Larry, for being the good sport he always was - he really loved Norman and Norman really loved his Dad. His brother and sister, Christopher and Kerry Lynn, adored him from the start. Our family and friends were inordinately patient with my inability to train a dog. In my defense, I got better with Norman, though, far from perfect! I always said I was great with children and hopelessly lost when it came to dogs. Norman never minded and somehow we all survived.

To this day I don't know what to do with my last bite of food - I always saved it for Norman. He would never beg, but would patiently await that small morsel, and favor me with a satisfied glance after I finally forked it over.

B-B-BAD TO THE BONE

Norman

The sheet of ice had formed on our back deck during a snowstorm. Norman discovered he could play with these pieces of ice, lick them, and then toss them down the deck, all the while chasing them like he would any other toy. One morning he decided he'd like to bring the piece inside. I quickly read his mind.

"Absolutely not." I said.

But Norman proceeded to try and figure out how to get that huge chunk of frozen water in through his doggie door. The ice was bigger than Norman; about three feet across and held in his mouth like the limb of a tree. It took him almost half an hour before he finally figured out if he just turned it the other way it would easily fit in the small opening. He was so proud when he finally accomplished this task I didn't have the heart to take it from him, and he got the last laugh.

Shortly after he came inside with the ice, I was distracted trying to get two kids ready for school. I took the kids to school, and upon returning, Norman was comfortably chewing the large, solid block of ice, on the top of our bed. There was water everywhere, the bedspread, blankets and sheets were soaked and I don't think that bed dried for weeks. A little bit of ice goes a long way.

Our dear friends, Connie and Mike, had recently purchased a new home in Southern California. They spent almost as much on an incredible plan to landscape their new backyard as they did on the house. This plan included a new pool, spa, grass, palm trees, and an entire hill of flowering flora.

On one of our many trips down to visit, the weather turned and it began to rain. Connie and Mike's recently landscaped yard was under water. Norman was with us as we always brought him everywhere. Although not fond of water, Norman did have an unusual affinity for mud; wet, mushy, caked, dried or just there.

Mike had given strict instructions as to what and where Norman could go while outside. We tied him to a long lead and he had fun playing in the new yard before all hell broke loose, and I do mean loose. He broke free of that pesky lead. Connie and I happened to look out the window just in time to witness Norman tearing through their backyard like a crazed animal. He was really having fun.

Connie and I just laughed, poured more wine, and immediately started contriving a story for Mike. Norman, now a giant ball of wet mud eyed us looking at him and laughing. Before we could stop him he ran over to the sliding door, blew through the closed screen, tore it open and flopped his muddy rear end on top of Connie's new couch. I hope my face looked as horrified as Connie's.

Time stood still. The cleanup was nasty, took hours, it cost us money for a new screen door, and yet we still laughed. At least, we laughed until Mike came home. We saved Norman's life that night by hiding him in the car for a bit—Connie and I were not so lucky. A little bit of laughter makes mud go a long way.

Norman's last bit of craftiness happened just a few months ago. Our son, Christopher, home from overseas, noticed that when he let Norman out to roam around the house he'd return with food of some sort. A little backstory on Norman; he was a chowhound. There was never a morsel of food that got by him. Honestly, that dog would have eaten himself to death if allowed.

So there were two questions. Why was the dog bringing home the food, intact, and where was he getting it? We live in a very remote neighborhood with only a few homes. Norman never went farther than next door so that's where we figured he was acquiring these groceries. After speaking with our neighbors we were even more puzzled as none of them said anything was missing. Day after day Norman would show up with items like a whole chicken, a bag of flour and even a couple of loaves of unopened bread. Chris and I laughed and laughed about what would show up next - we even tried following him to see where he was getting this food.

We never really solved the mystery but did discover that out neighbors across the road were missing some bread after a trip to the market. Apparently Norman would wait until they went up their stairs then pop into their car and help himself to their groceries. I made Chris take Norman back over and apologize! A little bit of food goes a long way.

A Trip to Costco

Phoebe was our dog for many years before Norman came along. Our first large dog, Buddy, a Golden Retriever, was recently deceased and we began contemplating adding another dog into our growing family. As it turned out our friend, Cindy, was looking for a home for her recently purchased puppy. Her dog was a small, white Bichon Frisé, and her son was unable to tolerate the allergic reaction he got from being around her. We had never owned a small dog, we didn't understand the difference between a ten-pound Bichon and an eighty-pound Golden Retriever, but we were destined to find out! Our lives with Phoebe were filled with story after story of unbelievable antics, on her part, and even more unbelievable reactions on ours.

To say Phoebe was a character does her an injustice. That dog could make me angry, sad, lonely, happy, angry all over again, and still she made me laugh. The stories I relate are a mere fraction of the hijinks she participated in. Phoebe was one of a kind and was a remarkable addition to our family if for no other reason than the stories she left behind.

We live in a very remote area of Northern California. Just an outing to the grocery store takes a great deal of time and can be quite the adventure.

One day, I dropped the kids at school and decided to take our dog, Phoebe, with me as I drove 'down the hill' to shop at the closest Costco. It was an absolutely beautiful day, around 60 degrees, and the per-

13

fect weather to allow the dog to be with me and still be okay in the car while I shopped. But Phoebe did not care for being left alone. Period.

At the time we owned a Jeep. This vehicle had leather seats. Couple this fact with driving on winding mountain roads and this can be a disaster for a dog trying to keep their balance in the back seat. The dog would slide from one side of the car to the other as I drove around each curve. Needless to say, there was a great deal of whimpering going on behind me. Not sure what to do I finally settled on allowing Phoebe to sit in my lap.

I had become my own worst nightmare—one of those ladies who would drive around with their laps crowded by a fluffy dog, head hanging from the window, while the driver battled the steering wheel attempting to maintain control of the car. However, sometimes you just need to give in. Phoebe settled comfortably in my lap and we had an uneventful ride to Costco. The ride home was another story.

I had finally completed my shopping, rolled the cart towards the Jeep and noticed something funny. I had left all the windows opened a few inches and could actually hear Phoebe before I saw her. There was a very low growling sound coming from the vehicle even as I saw it shaking a bit. I was instantly worried something had happened to my dog as I quickly approached the Jeep. I opened the trunk and found my small, crazed, ivory colored dog covered in a sea of bright white fluffy, feathery material.

At this point, the mother of two young children, I was fully aware of how to childproof any space, and thought I had mastered dog proofing abilities, as well. I was sorely mistaken. Phoebe had enjoyed one solid hour to herself as she mischievously ripped to shreds one of my daughter's stuffed animals. Dismembered limbs were strewn everywhere, in a sea of white fluff from God knows where, sifting down from the roof of the car and over the dog's shoulders. It looked just like a small snowstorm hit the car while I was away. The storm had a name; Phoebe.

I was beyond furious. I battled a crazed and very happy dog, and ran interference as I tried to keep her in the car, all while frantically trying to unload the groceries. Fur was flying, feathers were floating, the dog was barking, and passers-by were enjoying the show. I managed to accomplish this task, get into the driver's seat only to remember the ride down.

It wasn't often I could outsmart a dog but I was confident I had, as I eyed the huge pile of Costco paraphernalia blocking the back seat, from the front. I was totally unprepared for the racket that followed almost all the way home. Phoebe, denied access to the front seat, had taken to vaulting up and over the back seat all the while barking and stirring up the white feathers still hanging in the air. I have no idea what this must have looked like to other cars passing by, but I didn't care. I was at my wits' end and just looked forward to getting home.

Almost an hour of this had frazzled my nerves and I wondered at the energy of such a small dog. Exiting the freeway, we began winding our way home. The barking stopped only to be replaced by whining and whimpering. As bad as I felt for Phoebe's distress I was secretly happy about the diminished noise level. A few minutes passed with blessed silence. I turned around a couple of times and watched as the dog had figured out how to stand up on the seat. She wedged herself by the door and was just looking out the closed window. Another few minutes passed and I noticed a large SUV approach from behind. The woman driving was clearly upset, I checked my speed, I was not going too slowly, and I started to try and find a turnout so she could pass. One appeared roughly a mile up the road and I pulled over. To my surprise she pulled up next to me and we both rolled down our windows.

Imagine, if you can, the Grey Poupon TV commercial. "Pardon me," one driver asks the other. "Do you have any Grey Poupon?" That commercial will give you a complete visual of my conversation with the distressed woman.

"Pardon me." She asked. "Do you have a small white dog?"

I answered yes, and quickly glanced over my shoulder. No Phoebe. Two things happened at once. I heard the woman say that a small, white dog had just blown out the back window of my car and I noticed a back window was opened all the way. Phoebe had apparently figured out how to roll down the automatic window. I looked again, no dog. I profusely thanked the woman as I put the car in park, opened the door and proceeded to run back the way I had come. I would have driven but there was simply nowhere to turn the car around. I knew this, and as I ran I was experiencing crushing guilt.

My dog knew nothing about cars, traffic, or roads. Only moments before I was daydreaming of how I could put a large pink bow on her, as I left her on the doorstep of the home of an unwitting wealthy person. I must have been a sight as cars veered around me; I looked like a wild haired woman running in the wrong direction, on a very dangerous and winding mountain road. I probably still had white feathers blowing behind me as I finally turned the bend and there, sitting by the roadside, was Phoebe.

All grievances aside, I was extremely happy and relieved to see she had only a scratch on her nose, no broken bones, and other than looking a bit puzzled, she looked pretty good. I, on the other hand, shook for an hour, as I could not rid the images of what could have happened to her, from my overly active imagination.

I carried that dog back to the car. I had left the keys and my purse in the car with the driver's door wide open. Everything was safe, the groceries were still there, and we were alive. Suffice it to say, I rarely took Phoebe on any more road trips.

Phoebe is long gone, but every time I pass that bend in the road I still see the image of my wild-eyed little pet just sitting there waiting for me to come get her. The memory of that day is still so vivid it tugs at my heart and still makes me laugh.

All That Glitters Is Not Gold

My sister, Terrie, rescued a five-month-old Lab named, Macy, several years ago. Macy is a shiny, jet black, beautiful and very tall dog. Did I say very tall? One great story comes from her, surrounding an evening event, with Macy and her other dog, Mollie.

Apparently Macy and Mollie had been out walking with Terrie, running and swimming, where they live at their cabin on a small island in the Great Northwest. Macy had ingested far too much of a particular seaweed she loved. It tasted good but wreaked havoc with her digestive tract and the end result was a night filled with intestinal turmoil and a ruined rug.

That evening, Macy threw up all over Terrie's newly purchased jute rug. An entire week of scrubbing and drying this rug left it very clean but unfortunately forever stained. Being the trooper she was Terrie decided to paint the soiled rug a la something she had learned from reading Martha Stewart's magazine. For this she chose metallic gold paint. Knowing the capacity of her dog's ability to gain access to forbidden items she had placed the gold paint very high up on a shelf far and away from Macy's ability to access it. Or so she thought.

A few days later and at the end of a long day, Terrie decided to take a shower, confident that all was secure in her cabin. No more than a few minutes into her shower she sensed something amiss. She got out of the shower, wrapped only in a towel, horrified to discover Macy, comfortably relaxed, and playing in a pool of gold metallic paint, on her very expensive blue couch. Her first thought was what a beautiful scene; sleek, black dog lounging on an expensive, aqua couch, all marinating in a pool of glittering, gold paint! The way she describes what happens next is beyond amazing.

Trying to get Macy away from the paint and the couch, Terrie lunges towards the dog, her towel drops away, and she is now buck naked in front of the very public picture window, positioned facing the street, front and center, in the main room of her cabin. She is frantically attempting to accomplish two things; get the paint can away from Macy and to stop her dog from causing more destruction.

Completely unaware that neighbors were passing by on their evening walks, Terrie forged ahead pursuing a dog covered in beautiful gold paint. Macy was hurdling over furniture, tracking paint on top of newly laid hardwood floors, and circling around and around hallways now replete with, not only drips of metallic gold paint but matching gold paw prints. Gold paint was absolutely everywhere!

Terrie really never had a chance; Macy was always two steps ahead of her as she pranced through the cabin. Eventually she caught her beautiful, black dog, ditched the empty gold can, and began the on-going effort to clean up all the paint that had curiously covered everything except the jute rug for which it had been initially intended.

Terrie can be applauded for a few accomplishments that evening. First, she did not actually harm her dog, Macy. Macy still lives happily together with Terrie and Mollie. Second, she provided a great deal of entertainment for her fellow neighbors who still reminisce about her Gold Diggin' Dog, Macy, and the evening Terrie regaled them through her large, picture window. She was a shining example of a middle aged woman, in great shape by the way, capable of streaking through her cabin, vaulting over furniture and navigating slippery floors all the while totally naked and focused only on catching that crazy dog!

Curiously, to this day, Terrie still finds metallic gold paint in the most unusual places!

Andy and Lorrie

This book is primarily about funny, dogs I have known and loved. It would be incomplete without a serious nod to our family friend's dog, Andy, and to his owner and our good friend, Lorrie. It's not that Andy and the many stories revolving around him aren't funny enough, it's just that when you add Lorrie into the mix the humor becomes unbeatable.

To clarify the situation, Lorrie hates Andy and Andy pretty much spends his life trying to steer clear of Lorrie. Andy is a five-year-old Jack Russell Terrier and Lorrie is his owner. Left several years earlier by Lorrie's daughter, Melissa, Andy still resides with his family, and thus he lives with Lorrie, not by choice. Fortunately for Andy there are two other major players in his canine life. There's Ted, Andy's dad and Lorrie's husband, and Molly, their youngest daughter, and Andy's 'little sister'.

To better explain Andy's living arrangements, he has a lovely home in the woods of Northern California, close to South Lake Tahoe. He has squirrels, wild turkey, and deer to chase every morning as Lorrie lets him out the sliding glass door hoping to never set eyes on him again. Fortunately Lorrie teaches third graders all day so Andy's survival potential spikes during school hours. When Lorrie arrives home from a taxing day spent with little monsters (my words not hers), Andy steers clear. This is always a wise choice. As a matter of fact we can always tell when Lorrie is home because Andy will be out on the deck, by the front door. When Lorrie is in, Andy is out.

The reason for all this discord between Lorrie and Andy revolves around one conspicuously prominent substance; dog hair. Lorrie has a beautiful home, tucked in the mountains and situated on a lovely piece of wooded property. Lorrie is very proud of her clean and always uncluttered home. Returning daily from work the last thing she can handle is dog hair everywhere. Although I never see it, Lorrie's x-ray vision can detect it a mile away. Additionally, when the sun shines just right in the mountains, beaming in laser like precision through clear windows, every last speck of dirt shows up with monumental clarity. This always happens just about the time Lorrie appears home from work. She sits down and looks around at all the dog hair, not only evident on the floor, but also floating everywhere in the light all around her, and her blood boils.

Andy can read her mind. I know this because I've seen it. He cocks his little head, follows her eyes, tenses up as she turns towards him ready to yell, and then the little guy actually vanishes! I've never seen exactly where he disappears to, but rumor has it, he slips under the desk, in the office off the hallway.

Last spring Andy had a bad Bath Day. Lorrie decided that, not only was the dog hair in the house out of control, but that Andy was starting to smell like a dog. She let him know, in a very loud voice, that he smelled bad.

I think her exact words were "You stink!"

When you tell Andy he smells his little tail tucks between his legs and he gets his feelings hurt. He didn't get away fast enough this particular afternoon though, as Lorrie got the bright idea to give him a bath and then get rid of the source of all the dog hair; she decided to shave him.

I showed up as the bath had already ended and a small, apparently drowned and shaved large rat, blasted out the front door, down the stairs and into my arms. I could see by his eyes it was Andy. He was slick, wet, and shaved completely beyond recognition. I carried him inside, wrapped him up, and Lorrie proceeded to tell me about his bath and how hard he was to shave. You think? Andy calmed down and I managed to keep him away from Lorrie while I was there.

For the next few weeks, peace reigned in the kingdom as Andy had no hair to shed in Lorrie's house.

Revenge is sweet and Andy got his a few months later, hair grown back, and on an early morning walk with Lorrie. Secretly, I think she likes him more than she lets on.

We have a beautiful lake by our homes. It's an amazing resource and has many horse, biking, and walking trails. It also offers camping, boating, and fishing. All in all, it is just a great place to visit and enjoy. Many of us take advantage of these trails to walk our dogs while getting some fresh air and exercise. A group of friends asked if Lorrie wanted to join them for a walk. It was very early morning so she took off her pajamas and put on a sweatshirt and some sweatpants—no underwear.

She was planning to shower when she returned so she was not overly concerned about her appearance. She grabbed Andy, put him on a leash and off they went.

The campground by our lake was still pretty full of summer campers as Lorrie and the group of walkers headed towards the water. Apparently Andy was traipsing ahead of Lorrie and stepped on an underground hornet nest. Lorrie followed and as she passed over it the hornets swarmed both her and the dog. Andy beat feet to the water and Lorrie swatted hornets madly, even as she realized she needed to follow Andy to the lake. Her friends were all shouting at her to take her sweatshirt off as the bees were blanketing the entire back of it. So, as she ran she peeled off her top and decided to do the same with her sweatpants. Remember what I said about no underwear? She danced around, squirmed and wiggled, still swatting hornets and finally got her clothes completely off.

So this is the visual: a small dog and a completely naked woman, still wearing white socks and tennis shoes, both racing towards the lake all the while being chased by a bunch of really angry hornets. Lorrie says the last thing she remembers is quickly looking back to a very large group of people, some of them her friends, others just campers, laughing and hooting at the spectacle before them. It gets better. There were hornets still all over her clothes so she was unable to retrieve them. Her friends somehow managed to get her enough cover so they could return to their cars. It sometimes makes me wonder if Andy didn't know exactly what he was walking over that morning. Lorrie has never shaved him again!

Phoebe Moves to Santa Fe

By now, dear reader, you are well acquainted with our dog, Phoebe's, antics. This story actually happened shortly after she arrived as a new member of our family. We had recently experienced a financial meltdown, were forced to move back to our North County San Diego rental property, and this is where Phoebe entered the picture.

My old friend, Cindy, was the culprit. As mentioned earlier, her son could not tolerate Phoebe's saliva, as he was allergic to it. This is why she began trying to convince me that we all needed a new dog and she just happened to have the perfect one. She should be in sales. Fast forward a month and Phoebe was all ours. I still think back and ponder whether her son really was allergic–or did Cindy simply know better? I'll never know and I am certain she'll never tell.

My husband, Larry, accepted a job far away from home. He would be working in Santa Fe, New Mexico. This was very hard on all of us however, Phoebe could not have been happier. She absolutely hated Larry. She tolerated the kids, and life with our cat, Clancy, was a challenge.

When Phoebe arrived, all cute and fluffy white, our cat merely eyed me, stuck up his tail, and exited the room. Life for Clancy was never the same. I will give him this; he simply never gave in. I would walk by the two of them, the dog and the cat, while they were busy actually boxing each other! They did not tolerate one other and I'll hand it to Clancy, he fought the good fight.

After several months of being separated from Larry, we all decided to move to Santa Fe, procure a home, and deal with a new location rather than remain separated. Larry was already there so it was entirely up to me to re-locate the entire household, rent out our home, pack everything, arrange for movers, and then drive the kids and pets through the desert to our new location. It all sounds so easy. There is a reason Move is a four letter word.

Our dear family friend, and extremely good sport, Mary, volunteered to accompany us as cell phones were new, I didn't have one, and she did. Her husband, Gary, graciously encouraged Mary to accompany me as she was a great friend, and a wonderful source of emotional and mental support We packed the two kids and the dog and cat into our Volvo and never looked back. Phoebe was her usual pleasant self during the first leg of this adventure. She barked at everything, constantly leaped over the seats when simply bored, all the while tormenting our cat, Clancy, as she had him confined and all to herself. We were just entering the Arizona desert, when the car started to act up. Mary and I looked at each other and kept driving while eying the roadside signs that warned, "Under No Circumstance - Do Not Pick Up Hitchhikers." Apparently there was a maximum-security penal institution nearby. This inspired dread in me as the car was really beginning to shake and act weird.

Mary and I thought the Volvo might be over heating as the temperature outside was a balmy 114 degrees. I turned the air off to see if the car would respond, watched as both the kids and animals began to wilt, and decided better. All at once the temperature gage spiked and at the same time the tire blew. At least the mystery was solved and it only involved a flat tire–or so I thought. Pulling over directly under the shadow of the Do Not Pick Up Hitchhikers sign, Mary and I rolled down the windows, got out of the car and prepared to empty the trunk so we could access the jack and spare tire.

Big mistake. Phoebe eyed the open window and bolted out before we realized what she was up to. I swear I saw a satisfied look come over Clancy's face. I think he thought he was rid of her forever. Needless to say, we chased down Phoebe, threw her back into the car and had to keep the windows up enough so that she wouldn't escape again. It was now 120 degrees, Mary's cell phone had no service, and both the kids and the animal's eyes were beginning to roll into the backs of their heads. To this day I have never experienced such intense heat.

Suddenly a very pretty and obviously expensive red Corvette passed us going in the opposite direction. We noted it as it looked as out of place as we did. Several minutes later it came back, and pulled up in front of us. I was terrified! We were completely vulnerable and all I had was a sorry old canister of expired pepper spray. However, we did have Phoebe. As the man approached I let her out and grabbed my pepper spray. Phoebe, God bless her, ran up to that man and barked like she was a ferocious guard dog. He said he and his eight-year-old son had been at a Boy Scout convention and they had seen our predicament as they passed us by. The son got out and between the four of us we were able to get a spare on the car and make it into Phoenix, Arizona.

That afternoon was a nightmare all around. However, Phoebe was involved so there was always the potential for disaster and the laughter that usually followed. She did not disappoint.

We drove the car to a Sears's auto shop and asked if we could get a new tire. They would not allow us to leave the animals in the car so we took them to the adjacent mall and collapsed on a bench by the entrance. It was so cool inside and the wait was only estimated to be an hour or so. The security guard approached and took one look at Mary and me, decided better, turned around, and simply looked the other way as we had our cat and dog with us. Eventually Phoebe could not behave one moment longer; she began to bark at everyone, and I knew I had to ditch her somewhere. With great stealth I crept back to our car, dog on the leash, and opened the door while shoving her inside. I slipped away quickly returning to Mary and my family.

We were finally relaxed while we waited for the car to be ready. Shortly thereafter, we kept hearing what appeared to be a very annoying car alarm. We couldn't figure out why it wasn't turning off as it kept honking and honking. Several minutes went by and, over the loud honking, we could hear the request for the owner of a blue Volvo to please come to the auto shop, immediately. It took a couple of minutes for me to compute that this meant me. We all gathered our belongings and headed back out into the intense heat.

The car horn noise got louder as we approached our Volvo. The technician said it would have been another two hours to complete the tire change if not for the mayhem caused by Phoebe. We looked over at the Volvo and there, in the front seat standing as tall as possible was Phoebe, Protector of the Car, growling at anyone getting even marginally close to the vehicle, and all the while leaning on the steering wheel, continuously honking the horn. It had been her all along.

The auto shop guys changed the tire in record time, just to get us out of their hair. Mary, the kids, and I will never forget the visual of that small dog impatiently blaring the horn awaiting our return so we could all get back on the road.

We left Sears and headed up to Flagstaff where we were spending the night with my brother, Bill. We opened a crisply chilled and much needed bottle of chardonnay and tried to regale my brother with our recent adventure but, to this day, I really think he thought we were all suffering from heat stroke. After all, you just can't make this stuff up!

The Hair of the Dog

Already having related a couple of stories about Phoebe, not much else needs to be said about her capacity for getting into trouble. There are several stories about her throughout this book, as she provided our family with many years of entertainment, but this is probably our children's favorite. This story has been told and re-told by Christopher and Kerry Lynn, usually with a glass of wine in hand—as you will see this is very appropriate.

It was a Friday, on a cold winter evening in the mountains where we live, and I had experienced a particularly stressful week. As I have mentioned before, we live in a remote area and grocery stores are quite a distance away. That said, I really was trying to wind down from a week filled with problems, over-active kids, a husband working from home, life with an impossible dog, and generally just being over done. I decided the best way to decompress would be a cold glass of crisp chardonnay and a hot shower.

Dinner was over, dishes were done, and I was a free woman. Much to my dismay, I discovered I was completely out of wine. This was not good. I moseyed on out to the extra refrigerator we kept in the garage generally stocked with additional wine used only for emergencies. If this wasn't an emergency I don't know what would have been. To my horror I found no wine outside, either. What I did spy was an old, boxed container of white wine shoved into the back of the refrigerator. Could this be possible? Usually never stooping so low as to actually purchase boxed wine, or juice boxes as my friends call them, apparently I had, and here it was. I was looking heavenward thanking the Powers That Be as I grabbed that box and hurried inside.

I realized the silver bladder holding the boxed wine was almost empty–I said almost. I was able to cut open the bladder and actually drained what was left into a ten-ounce glass. I was ecstatic! I had exactly one glass of wine and I was going to really enjoy it. I headed down the hallway towards our bedroom, placed the wine on a table by my side of our bed, turned the water on, and proceeded to take a much needed relaxing hot shower. All I could think about was sitting down, relaxed, clean and comfortable, picking up my book, and drinking that one glass of wine. I exited the bathroom, dressed and prepared to relax when I noticed the glass of wine was completely empty. Two things went through my mind at once; either my husband had come in and gulped my wine while I was showering, or I had a bigger problem: one our two kids had suddenly taken a liking to boxed white wine. As it turns out it was neither.

Our son, Christopher, had a plaid comforter on his bed and whenever Phoebe would get into trouble this is where we would find her. As a matter of fact, many times I would see her on top of his bed before I discovered what she had actually done wrong. That night was no exception. Empty glass of wine in hand, I dejectedly walked down the hall honestly thinking my week must have been so bad that I had already gulped the wine and simply could not remember. I happened to glance into Christopher's room as I sadly walked down the hall and there, curled on the top of his bed, was Phoebe.

With my antennae up, it did not take long to put two and two together. I was surprised. I had been with Phoebe for years and she had never been interested in anything I was eating or drinking. Never. New paradigm! Apparently she helped herself to the entire contents of my one, coveted glass of white wine while I was showering. She had not left a single drop of evidence as there were no tell tale signs of a slurping dog; a tipped glass or puddles of fluid, or anything of the sort. With great stealth she had lapped up my entire glass of wine and then retreated down the hall to her place of refuge. Little did she know how a full, ten ounce glass of wine would affect her tiny, ten pound body.

Initially very angry with Phoebe for drinking my wine, I soon realized something was really wrong. My husband had fallen asleep on the same bed and both he and Phoebe were sound asleep. The only difference being Phoebe was not snoring–yet. I called for Chris and Kerry Lynn and told them what she'd done and we all looked at each other puzzled as to what should be done. Chris burst into action. He called Phoebe's name and she could barely lift her head as she drunkenly tried to respond. I know this sounds cruel but, at the time, it was funny. Chris put her on the floor and she was, of course, to inebriated to walk, so we took her away from the snoring Dad and placed her in our family room while we pondered what to do. We lived so far from everything we decided we could attend to her that night and then, if need be, take her to the Vet's the next day.

The rest of that night was filled with laughter as I soon realized Phoebe was okay and had just had too much to drink. We watched her like a hawk. She slept, sometimes snoring, in my lap that evening, and in the morning was groggy and a bit subdued. I did call the Vet at that point, but he said she would be fine. He asked me to be sure she drank lots of water and to be sure she ate normally that day.

During Phoebe's really bad morning, my friend Connie called just to check in. Telling her the story of what had happened the night before I was unable to stop her from laughing long enough to even finish giving her an update on how Phoebe was doing. Before I cold relate to her how hung over the dog was she already had a solution. Her idea was to fill Phoebe's dish with a bit of beer–she called it the 'Hair of the Dog.' Of course I did not comply but once again we had a great laugh.

We wondered in utter amazement at Phoebe's ability to survive just about anything and appreciated the fact she had provided yet another ridiculous story to remember.

Expensive Christmas Kisses

Several years ago we experienced a family emergency that would require all of us to travel 500 miles, from our home in the woods of Northern California, to Southern California. Immediate arrangements were made and, you guessed it, Phoebe, our small Bichon Frisé, was going to be 'abandoned' for over one week. Our friend's children, Mary and Mike, agreed to help watch the house, take care of the dog and cat, and generally make sure Phoebe was entertained, fed and monitored.

It was Christmastime and I had purchased many gifts and wrapped them for mailing. Each year we would give our six nephews and one niece a twenty-dollar bill, usually wrapped around some form of Christmas candy. That year, I had chosen red and green foil covered Hershey kisses. They sat in a large, see through, plastic candy cane. I wrapped the twenty-dollar bills around the top of each large container, tied them with a beautiful bow, labeled them, and then tripled wrapped them in plastic bags. I did this so the dog could not smell them and thus not get near them or worse, actually eat them. This worked fine and for a couple of weeks, as I compiled other gifts to add to the pile of items to mail, Phoebe would occasionally eye the growing pile of gifts but she showed complete ambivalence towards the burgeoning mound.

As I said before, we needed to leave town quickly and I was able to hire Mary and Mike to watch Phoebe and the house. From what Mary told me upon our return, all had gone well while we were away, until that last day.

Apparently Phoebe had dealt with enough in terms of her family disappearing on her. She presumably experienced an all out DEF-CON 4 meltdown, decided to get inventive in terms of entertaining herself, and went ballistic the evening we were to return. Bless her heart, Mary tried to clean the disaster area but to no avail.

She still remembers that evening and her crushing, but unwarranted guilt; as far as I know, she did her very best in dealing with Phoebe's latest escapade.

Fast forward to our family returning from a really difficult week, a drive of over 500 miles and an eight-hour day spent together in the car. We were all beyond tired and completely unprepared for what was awaiting us as we all thankfully piled in the front door. We actually could not believe our own eyes!

Phoebe greeted us at our front door. She barked happily when she saw us and could barely contain herself. We walked immediately into our living room, dodging a frenzied dog, and stopped cold. As far as we could see into the kitchen, through the dining room and way back into the family room, we witnessed giant, basketball sized brown spots, all topped off with a pile of still shiny, green and red metallic Hershey Kisses wrappers, beautifully arranged and sitting pretty on top. As if this was not unbelievable enough each suspicious looking puddle sported a dirty yet curiously still recognizable twenty-dollar bill. Not to swift on my feet after the long drive, it took me several moments to process what exactly was all over our house. The kids groaned, as they smelled it first. It was recycled chocolate.

I looked over at what appeared to be a very proud Phoebe, sitting by one of her piles of regurgitated chocolate kisses. My first thought was concern for her as I knew chocolate was pure poison to a dog. Not so Phoebe. Not only had she eaten all the Christmas candy but she had apparently felt it necessary to ingest all the twenty-dollar bills as well. Evidently all the plastic, colored foil wrappers and Hershey Kisses did not agree with her delicate digestion.

Really?

Once again, too late to call our vet, I convinced myself that she would be okay as she had obviously consumed all these gifts hours before, she was still remarkably alive and she was acting as crackbrained as usual. Curiously I initially felt compelled to pick out all the money and wash them several times in hot, soapy water. I think I even ran them through the dishwasher a couple of times. Eventually I traded them with my husband for brand new ones. What he did with the old ones I'll never know.

That night I was able to partially clean up most of the stained spots on the floor and furniture though this activity took hours as Phoebe scrupulously supervised my every move. She was inordinately proud of her mischief and seemed puzzled by my inability to have fun while cleaning up all her hard work. She managed to drag out what remained of the plastic candy canes and even played with them as I scrubbed and scrubbed.

I finally needed to stop as I was exhausted and I set out the phone book so I would remember to call our Carpet Cleaner the following day. The chocolate was simply not coming out of the carpet or the furniture. Eventually, including the added expense of carpet cleaning–along with replacing the original gifts–those plastic candy canes wound up being worth sixty-five dollars each!

Within the week I was able to mail the new gifts, which all arrived just in the nick of time for Christmas.

This was to be Phoebe's last performance as she left us shortly thereafter. Honestly, to this day I still have an instant visceral reaction when I see a small, white Bichon Frisé. My back tenses up, my mouth goes dry and I notice my heart beating a bit more quickly. Then I remember it's not my wild and insanely crazy little dog. Sometimes I will stop the owners and ask about any shenanigans they may have experienced with their small Bichons. Curiously, most of them look at me with a look of puzzled innocence. Apparently, I am the only person on this planet who has ever had any trouble with her little pet. To listen to all these other owners you'd think their dogs were virtual saints. I am convinced they are either in serious denial or, more likely, simply not talking!

DOUBLE-TROUBLE

Royal Double Trouble

Our cousin, Patty, provided me with my initial introduction to the antics of small dogs. Even before I was married, I witnessed the hijinks of her two adorable and ever entertaining little dogs, royally named Squire and Duchess. These names were beyond appropriate as this dynamic duo could also be as much royal entertainment as a royal pain in the rear end! It was primarily how they interacted that brought such laughter and enjoyment to everyone.

Squire was a small gray, Cairn Terrier who had a curious relationship with the household's gas heater. Visitors to Patty's home, having heard of Squire's offbeat habit, would patiently wait in anticipation for the heater to fire up and Squire would immediately mobilize into frenzied action.

This ritual would start by Squire actually opening the door to the cupboard, where the appliance was, and then wait, perfectly still until it completely turned on. Heater fully blazing, Squire would begin growling at it incessantly even as he would race from room to room barking at all the heat registers, located on the floor of each and every room. All action would suddenly cease as soon as the heat turned off. Apparently it was the hot air that he enjoyed chasing (no editorial comment on all the hot air in Patty's household).

Curious to the rest of us observing was what could be found inside this gas heater closet. I would not have believed it had I not seen it with my own eyes. Squire thought of this as his closet. Located on the small shelf a couple of inches from the floor, were an entire array of doggie toys all lined up in a perfectly straight row. I kid you not; squeakies, bones, and even small matchbox cars were all neatly placed where only he could find them. He finished the entertainment, while still eyeing all of us watching in utter disbelief, by shoving the heater closet door shut as he padded outside to chase the shadows of the airplanes flying overhead. Squire's work was never done.

Duchess entered the scene a few years later and put Squire's mischief to shame. This dog's middle name was Trouble with a capital T. Patty thought of her as part dog, part cat, and part human. She was a small Shih Tzu whose motto was Relocation, Redistribution and Rediscovery.

It was Duchess' personal mission to bring all things inside outside and vice versa. In order to accomplish this she needed to master the doggie door. Many times during the course of the day Patty would find her little trouble-maker, toy in mouth, hanging half in and half out of the small opening, annoyingly suspended and restricted by it's rubber flap. She was so tiny that, as she tried to play and run after Squire, she'd get stuck somewhere in the middle of the doggie opening. This was one of Squire's revenge tactics and he used it daily, and generally whenever he was just plain bored. Once outside, Duchess would bring into the house all sorts of great stuff; flowers, rocks, stems, twigs and various debris. Many times during the day Patty would witness her small pet with a mouthful of colorful flowers, dirt and greens, yet again suspended from the doggie door, squirming and whimpering for rescue, and roll her eyes as she simply passed by wishing her well.

Eventually Duchess mastered the doggie door, however, she never stopped her sincere Redistribution efforts. Together Squire and Duchess entertained each other as much as they were very busy all day long and double trouble personified.

Squires other bit of retaliation towards Duchess involved Patty's new treadmill. He was inordinately pleased one Christmas when this shiny, new exercise device magically appeared in the family room. It was placed in front of the large picture window and right next to the beautifully decorated Christmas tree. We were never sure exactly how Squire taught Duchess to 'ride' the treadmill but it provided much laughter and amusement. As Patty would begin exercising, Duchess would jump up on the front of the machine with her and directly onto belt. She would glide between Patty's feet and lickety-split be rolled off the treadmill, then quickly whiz across the hardwood floor, into the well-lit Christmas tree. Squire would simply sit quietly by, little head cocked to the side, and only move his noggin as he watched Duchess fly by at breakneck speed. He never moved as lights jangled, bells jingled and ornaments dropped and clanked onto the hardwood floor. He looked only mildly interested as Duchess kept repeating her adventure until Patty would stop walking and carefully redistribute the lights along with picking up the decorations spread all over the room. Duchess would stop, shake her head a couple of times and simply pad off to find some other form of trouble to engage in. Inevitably, Squire would hear the gas heater in his private toy closet fire up and he'd head into the kitchen to await his job of monitoring all the household hot air.

The rest is history and you know the drill!

Cheri and Toto - There's No Place Like Home

This is another story where the combined escapades of adorable dogs make for a great 'doggy tale.' Many years ago, I had never even heard of the dog breed Bichon Frise, much less met one. This experience was to presage my future and–had I paid more attention–I probably never would have ended up with our little Bichon, Phoebe. However, my introduction to this Bichon, Cheri, and her antics, was not only hilarious, but also led to my introduction to a woman I still consider to be a dear friend, a mentor, and the big sister I never had. Without Peggy, so many avenues in my life would never have opened and her constant encouragement to expand my artistic horizons was responsible for all my current success. She and her beautiful family were our next-door neighbors for years and this is where our story begins.

Our little family had just moved into an incredible neighborhood by the sea, in Redondo Beach, California. The children were very young, Christopher was four and Kerry Lynn was two. The immediate area sported beautiful, cottage-like homes, winding wooded roads, and a quiet and peaceful atmosphere all delightfully accompanied by the faint background music of the nearby ocean. While we were still unpacking I allowed the kids to play out in the front yard. It was a large space, as it combined two grassy areas–ours and our neighbor's.

In a yard custom made for kids, mine were out having a blast. They were cheerily and with great abandon hurling clods of dirt at one another. I yelled out for them to find something less messy to toss around and Christopher asked if they could go next door to play with their new friends, Jimmy, Greg, and Kevin. I watched them go in through the back gate of our neighbor's home and felt surprisingly jealous of their free time. I had at least one million boxes to unpack and I was not looking forward to any of it.

Shortly thereafter, I saw and then heard quite the spectacle. Apparently my son, Christopher, had either left our neighbor's back gate opened or simply allowed their dog, Cheri, out of her confines, into the front yard and the street. The kids were all out playing in that yard when a large Animal Control truck screeched into the curb. A seemingly very angry, huge woman stormed out of the truck and started arguing with my new neighbor, Peggy.

I was inside and behind a substantial sized picture window so I was unable to really make out what was going on outside. However, delighted at any distraction that would allow me to stop unpacking the myriad boxes before me, I was happy to meander on out to the sunny porch and attempt to look like I was seriously minding my own business. I sat down on the step, listened and heard my neighbor, Peggy, lose her temper. Recollecting, this would be the first and last time I would ever hear Peggy actually raise her voice.

It was later I would discover that their dog, Cheri, was a Great Escape Artist. Seemingly taking advantage of any and all avenues of escape, she would simply disappear, sometimes daily, and inevitably Peggy would get a call from Animal Control to come on down and pick up her mischievous dog. This afternoon was different as Cheri was actually in the yard and the Animal Control Officer was trying to give a ticket to Peggy. The argument was that the dog had been in the street without a license and deserved punishment for this horrifying offense. The woman was threatening to take the dog if Peggy did not fork over a check for the ticket.

Easy for Peggy, she simply said, "Fine. I don't want the dog. Take the dog." This angered the woman further as Cheri wiggled and whimpered trying to simply get down and get into trouble anywhere else but where she was. The progressively heated conversation went like this:

"You take the dog!"

"I don't want the dog."

"It's your dog!"

"I don't want the dog, you can have the dog!"

Peggy's final argument was, "How can you ticket me for something that has already happened? By the time you arrived," she emphatically insisted, "the dog was back in her own yard."

I instantly sided with my new neighbor and had to keep quiet, as I wasn't even supposed to be listening. I did manage to loudly clap as the Animal Control Officer huffed and puffed and got back into her ridiculously over-sized truck. That lady had too much taxpayer time on her hands. Cheri was immediately put back into her yard where, in all probability, she was preliminarily planning the details of her next breakout.

Did I mention breakout? What happened next was a result of the relationship and combination of two dogs, one Cheri, the other Toto, and several shared events. As it happened, Peggy took in a little Norfolk Terrier, named Toto. She was a temporary addition to their household as this poor, little pup was consistently shuffled between families, never really landing anywhere for good. Her owners were constantly in motion, moving and relocating, thus she was sort of a serially abandoned little dog (personal aside–some people should never be allowed to have a dog).

Anyway, bless Peggy's heart, she took in this neglected, little Terrier and did her best to make her life as pleasant as possible. Cheri, on the other hand, had other ideas about Toto's future, and a completely different agenda in mind for this new and Unwanted Interloper.

Fast forward to countless days with Cheri beginning the same as many before. Currently the only difference was Toto. Numerous times prior to this, Cheri had escaped her confines but these days were different, as she took Toto with her. Nothing was unusual on this particular day as Cheri exited the backyard with an unsuspecting Toto innocently trailing behind. This was certainly not the first time Cheri had led Toto out of the safety of their yard and into the wilds of Redondo Beach. Cheri was constantly attempting to ditch Toto but was inevitably unsuccessful as Toto was used to being ditched.

Due to the fact that Toto was 'visiting,' Peggy had simply put an old collar of Cheri's around Toto's neck and never thought any more about it that is, until she kept getting calls from people asking her to come and get her dog, Cheri. Apparently Cheri's "ditch and abandon" agenda had been temporarily successful yet Toto always managed to find her way home and many times way before Peggy needed to go pick her up from wherever the phone call had generated. However, Cheri prevailed and this last interaction ended well but, as it turns out, caused a lot of unnecessary concern and worry.

It was on a weekday when Peggy realized Cheri had been missing again and they started the usual round of calls only to see her eventually walking up the street looking extremely satisfied and utterly alone - no Toto. Fortunately, many hours later, after dinner, a neighbor from several blocks away called to say they had their dog, Cheri (really Toto). Curiously they stated that they had seen a small white Bichon 'drop' Toto off in their yard. Toto stuck around because there were children laughing and playing who enjoyed and welcomed her. They noted that the other dog sort of slithered away, almost like she wanted to abandon Toto. You think?

These people were kind enough to entertain Toto who seemingly had no desire to return home. They fed her dinner and continued calling for someone to come retrieve 'Cheri'. However, one of the kids kept picking up the calls and would turn only to see the real Cheri relaxing on the family room couch and thus understandably ignore the request. These were very young boys, mind you, and the person on the phone kept referring to the dog in question as Cheri. Finally, the last time one of the boys answered the phone, unaware that it was Cheri's old collar circling Toto's neck, he simply gave up in confusion as Cheri was right there behind him, head cocked curiously to one side, innocently sitting pretty on their comfortable couch. Problem solved. Cheri was home and not missing.

However, as the evening progressed the neighbors persisted in calling. Finally, after a couple more attempts, the kids stopped picking up the phone and Peggy answered speaking with them herself. She quickly solved the problem. She knew it was Toto, wearing Cheri's old collar, that they were talking about and obviously not Cheri. In the meantime, Peggy turned to see a very smug and curiously satisfied looking Cheri. She had never budged from her prominent position, remaining perched on the cozy couch, thinking she had successfully and finally rid her family of that Beastly Toto!

As in all great sagas, Toto found her way home and eventually was placed with a loving and permanent family far away and forever safe from Cheri. Peggy was sad to see Toto go but happy Cheri had not succeeded in abandoning her forever. Toto finally discovered there really was no place like home, a new home!

Doggie Tales from the Dynamic Duo

My husband and I have two, very dear friends, Marcia and Dennis, who are always extra fun to spend time with as they usually have an entertaining array of pets around to amuse us. Dennis still loves to tease me about my abysmal success at any form of dog training so I particularly enjoy relaying the following stories revolved around the antics of two of their 'perfectly trained' canines!

Marcia and Dennis really love Weimaraners. Two of their favorites lived, loved, and played together for many years. Emma and Teufel were one and a half years apart and they were astoundingly beautiful dogs, a glorious color of silvery gray, with delightfully soft fur and wonderful temperaments. Once again, separately they were funny but together they provided many years of amusing stories.

Emma was a gorgeous female and she knew it. Marcia describes her as a bit haughty but I would defend Emma's haughtiness as she provided the brains for all their shenanigans.

Teufel, which is the German word for devil, was a handsome male. Marcia and Dennis both described Teufel as a large, lovable oaf. I believe their affectionate nickname for him was 'Dufus'. Emma was the brain of the Dynamic Duo and Teufel was the brawn. All mischief was pursued strictly as a team and all credit for any antics were equally shared.

Generally well behaved and perfectly trained (that was for you, Den), these guys were inclined to get into trouble due to one simple thing - they were bored. Marcia and Dennis would daily leave for work secure in the knowledge that their dogs were safely inside the double garage and attached to a completely accessible doggie door. This doggie door opened out into a securely fenced dog run. However, both Emma and Teufel soon learned how to escape. Apparently together they figured out how to open the door to the house with their teeth.

Marcia and Dennis realized this as the door and solid metal door-knob were severely mangled by suspicious teeth marks. They solved this problem by installing a new deadbolt. This did not discourage the dogs and the damage to the door and knob increased, however, they felt reasonably proud, being the smarter of the two species, that they had resolved the issue. The dogs definitely stopped getting into the house.

Savoring their victory and always finding Emma and Teufel still in the garage where they had left them each morning, Marcia and Dennis were extremely puzzled as they kept getting calls from their neighbors. These neighbors occasionally reported they would see the two dogs wandering together around the neighborhood only to return home when they were tired.

Each time this happened they would come home from work and the automatic and very large garage door would be wide opened. After major sleuthing and observing the telltale scratch marks, they really believed that the two dogs had figured out how to jump up and push the opener to the garage door. Seemingly unbelievable, they decided that one of the dogs, Emma, had discovered that she could hit—initially by accident and thereafter intentionally—the garage door button that was about head high and to the right of the door leading from the garage into the house. They assumed Emma had taught Teufel this dastardly trick so they set up a test in order to catch them. They secured a wire basket over the button and miraculously the dogs stopped escaping. Problem solved, or so they thought. The dogs' prowess with doors was not limited to typical doorknobs; when they were at home with the dogs, they would routinely find one of their French doors opened, usually the one leading into the back yard.

They always suspected Emma and Teufel, but were never successful at actually witnessing this suspected and extraordinary talent. After an extended period of time Marcia finally caught Emma red handed, at the door. She would gracefully stand up on her two back paws and gently press lightly on the levered door handle with her front right paw. Then Emma would drop back down quietly on all fours and she and her accomplice, Teufel, would exit and be off on yet another adventure.

Not long after Marcia and Dennis stopped Emma and Teufel from playing with the garage door opener, they moved to another home in Laguna Beach, California. They had a perfect walled in driveway connected to a separate garage creating a safe space and a large dog run for both dogs. However, one side of the driveway was constructed as a three-foot brick wall topped with lattice. The wall was completely encumbered by a heavy, weeping fig tree with vines reaching up around ten feet high. Undaunted, Teufel insisted on chewing through the lattice and heavy vines on multiple occasions. For a while, the more Dennis patched the holes, the more places the two dogs would find to chew through the fence and breakout.

Typically on the days they escaped, they ran into neighbors who would kindly replace them in their yard where they stayed put for the rest of the day. On a not-so-typical breakout day Marcia and Dennis had left town for brunch with our mutual and very dear friends, Judy and John. Just as they were returning, they received a call saying that guests who were staying at the Pacific Edge Hotel, on the Coast Highway, in Laguna Beach, had captured their dogs.

They told them they had watched these two, beautiful and curiously unmonitored dogs cross the extremely busy four lane highway, totally unsupervised, even as they followed them down the walkway, to the beach. They watched as the dogs joyfully romped around, played in the waves, chased each other, chased other dogs and generally had a blast. These kind and concerned people attempted to corral them but to no avail.

Having had enough beach time the Dynamic Duo of Emma and Teufel moseyed on back the way they had come and this is where they were finally nabbed. Serious bribery involving lots of food was successfully employed, they called Marcia and Dennis and everyone went home. Shortly thereafter Dennis was able to completely patch the fence and thus all avenues of future escape. Eventually, they quit even trying to escape and peace reigned in the Forsyth household.

Even in their later years these two dogs provided entertainment. Emma and Teufel were in their senior years, Teufel was twelve and Emma thirteen, when Marcia and Dennis decided to try leaving them in the house while they went out for dinner with some friends. After all it was cold outside, their antics had pretty much subsided and guilt dominated what would turn out to be better judgment. Arriving home they both realized their pesky Dynamos had been very busy indeed. Walking in the front door they were equally amused then dismayed as they saw toilet paper absolutely everywhere. The streaming white strands trailed from the downstairs bathroom, around all the rooms, into the hall, and even up the stairs. Marcia and Dennis were pretty sure it was Emma's idea but equally certain that it was Teuful who pulled off the TP job. The next hour was spent picking up toilet paper and chasing down two frisky dogs that were still happy to terrorize their owners!

Emma and Teufel were wonderful dogs, great companions and truly an amazing and Dynamic Duo.

Conclusion

Explanations for a book's title are usually found in the beginning of a book, maybe in the Introduction or the Dedication. I chose to conclude this small offering of amusing stories with an explanation of why the title of this group of stories is named as it is, and why it means so much to me.

When Norman was diagnosed with cancer we chose a middle of the road approach, in terms of treatment for his disease, entertaining hopes of retrieving his health and at least keeping him comfortable and pain free. We were unable to cure him but we were successful in extending his life a bit, though not long enough, and I truly believe he never really suffered. I figured as long as he was still acting normally, playing, eating, drinking, and eliminating, this demonstrated that he was okay for the time being. Norman and I had many heart-to-heart discussions about the timing of how we would end his suffering and I knew he'd let me know when it was time for me to gracefully allow him to leave.

This book is supposed to make you feel better, dear reader, so I won't go into the nasty details of Norman's last couple of days as everyone who has ever lost a dog knows this process all too well.

The weekend prior to Norman's death, Connie and Mike were up at our home to watch the Superbowl with our family. I felt like I was cheating Connie, as I was simply unable to socialize and party as usual. She knew my heart was aching for my beloved dog and being the amazing friend she is, Connie never complained even as she helped me feed the dog and attend to his medications. Norman was actually okay that weekend. He was eating and he thankfully perked up around our dear, old friends, and seemed genuinely happy.

When Connie and Mike returned home the following Monday, Norman began to show disinterest in any food.

Even though I fully understood what was ahead, I purchased some baby food, and he seemed interested in that for a couple of meals. By Tuesday morning, after being up all night attending to him, we eyed each other and I just knew. He was uninterested in anything to eat–a bad indicator–and he looked at me with such compassion and longing.

I know this sounds insane and a bit unbelievable but I knew what that dog was thinking. He was sticking around for me not for himself. After I tried one last desperate attempt at feeding him I called our wonderful veterinarian, Karen, and she said to just bring him on down.

Originally she had agreed to come to our home however, this was not going to work as I didn't have the strength or enough people around to help me dig a grave and transport a ninety-two pound dog gracefully into the ground next to his beloved cat, Clementine. This broke my heart but I knew what had to be done. Norman and I drove around for a bit with me talking incessantly to him, letting my constant companion of nine years know how much I loved him and that he was simply the Best Dog Ever.

When we walked into the Vet's office, the entire staff joined us and Norman was given a drug to relax him into sleep prior to the kill shot. It was at that point our Vet came in, greeted him cheerfully and he actually jumped up to greet her. He loved that woman.

She said what she always said to him. "Norman, do you want a cookie?" I was shocked to see him jump up, happy and eager to take the cookie and chow it down! Tearful laughter ensued. Shortly thereafter when it was all over, I was beyond grief and called Connie to tell her all the sordid details. She listened patiently and when I came to the part about Norman eating the cookie, with her usual ability to encapsulate any situation into an amusing phrase, she compassionately laughed.

"Oh Debbie, how wonderful." Connie told me. "Norman took A Cookie To Go!"

Last But Not Least

Thank you for purchasing this little book. So many people have gratefully responded that these stories truly got them through a difficult time and others simply really enjoyed the hilarious antics of the dogs I have known and loved. They were also generous in their thanks as they were pleased and able to share this book with friends who had recently lost a beloved companion. My proposition to you is this: send me at least one funny story about one of your dogs, past or present, consistent along the lines of what you have read in this book, and I will consider it for publication in my next book dedicated to the readers of this fist one. I want my second set of stories to be yours! It will be called "A Cookie To Go - Stories From You".

As I have probably not admitted I am, by trade, a fine artist. I am an oil painter and would love to share my art with you, as well. Please feel free to visit my website at www.djkiggins.com to view my artwork. While there you can also order additional copies of this book. If you'd like them hand-signed or sent as a gift let me know. I'm happy to do either. Contact information can be found there, as well.

God Bless, dear reader, and for those who have lost their wonderful companion, I truly believe that somewhere your precious pet is simply awaiting your return.

www.ingramcontent.com/pod-product-compliance
Lightning Source LLC
Chambersburg PA
CBHW030543290526
45786CB00004B/1842